Delegating to Achieve Results

Robert B. Maddux

CRISP PUBLICATIONS, INC.
Los Altos, California

Delegating to Achieve Results

Robert B. Maddux

CREDITS
Editor: **Tony Hicks**
Designer: **Carol Harris**
Typesetting: **Interface Studio**
Cover Design: **Carol Harris**
Artwork: **Ralph Mapson**

Printed in the United States of America

English language Crisp books are distributed worldwide. Our major international distributors include:

CANADA: Reid Publishing, LTD., Box 7267, Oakville, Ontario Canada L6J 6L6. TEL: (416) 842-4428, FAX: (416) 842-9327

AUSTRALIA: Career Builders, P. O. Box 1051, Springwood, Brisbane, Queensland, Australia 4127. TEL: 841-1061, FAX: 841-1580

NEW ZEALAND: Career Builders, P. O. Box 571, Manurewa, Auckland, New Zealand. TEL: 266-5276, FAX: 266-4152

JAPAN: Phoenix Associates Co., Mizuho Bldg. 2-12-2, Kami Osaki, Shinagawa-Ku, Tokyo 141, Japan. TEL: 443-7231, FAX: 443-7640

Selected Crisp titles are also available in other languages. Contact International Rights Manager Tim Polk at (415) 949-4888 for more information.

Library of Congress Catalog Card Number 89-81246
Maddux, Robert B.
Delegating to Achieve Results
ISBN 1-56052-008-6

PREFACE

One of the most difficult tasks for supervisors (especially new ones), is learning to apportion the work among the employees they supervise. The difficulty is often due to just those personal qualities—job knowledge, competent personal performance, initiative, motivation, and a reasonable degree of interpersonal skills—that made them successful employees in the first place and ultimately led to their promotion. Those qualities might lead new supervisors to believe they can do all the important work in their unit by themselves.

These qualities may have made the employee successful in the past, but they can become a heavy burden if they are misapplied in the supervisory role. The new supervisor must contrast the old assignment with the new, and identify the critical differences. One of the most important differences is this: since the new task is too much for one person to accomplish, other employees have been assigned to help. They bring skills and knowledge in varying degrees and expect to use them and develop them. So the supervisor is responsible not only for his or her performance, but also for the performance and development of his or her subordinates. Their combined efforts are required to accomplish the goals and objectives of the unit.

The supervisor must recognize the role change from performing tasks to managing the performance of others. Concentration must now focus on planning, organizing, motivating, and controlling. This requires learning new skills and backing away from doing tasks that can be done by subordinates. The supervisor must learn to delegate and do it well.

If the skills of delegation are not learned and polished at every opportunity, success will be limited and the likelihood of promotion will be low. Those with limited delegation skills who are promoted will find their new jobs extremely difficult, and they will ultimately have a negative impact on the productivity of their unit.

Delegation is not some mysterious art available to only a chosen few. It is a basic management process that can be learned and honed to a fine edge by anyone who is willing to make the effort and able to get some practice. Providing the principles is what this book is about. Applying them is up to you. Good luck!

Robert B. Maddux

CONTENTS

SOME IMPORTANT OBJECTIVES FOR THE READER

Before you begin this book, give some thought to your objectives.

Objectives give us a sense of direction, a definition of what we plan to accomplish, and a feeling of fulfillment when they are achieved.

Check the objectives below that are important to you. Then, when you have completed this book, review your objectives and enjoy the sense of achievement you will feel.

AFTER LEARNING AND PRACTICING THE CONCEPTS PRESENTED IN THIS BOOK, YOU WILL BE ABLE TO:

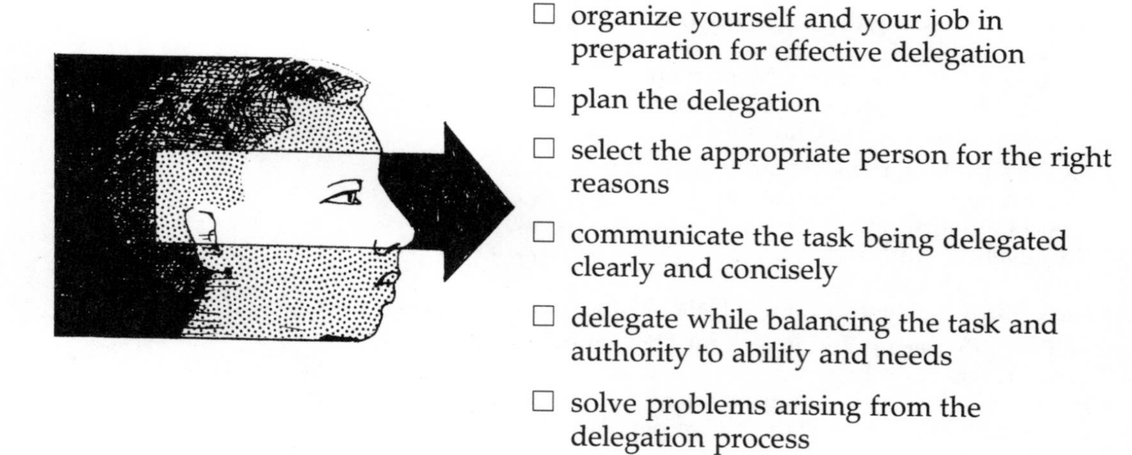

- ☐ organize yourself and your job in preparation for effective delegation
- ☐ plan the delegation
- ☐ select the appropriate person for the right reasons
- ☐ communicate the task being delegated clearly and concisely
- ☐ delegate while balancing the task and authority to ability and needs
- ☐ solve problems arising from the delegation process

PART

I

The Role of the Manager

MANAGEMENT IS A PROCESS

> Management is the process of working through individuals and groups to accomplish organizational goals and objectives.

When a person assumes a managerial position there is a distinct change in that person's relationships with other employees, and a whole new set of tasks begin to unfold. These tasks, taken together, are generally referred to as the management process.

Management practioners and scholars vary widely in their definitions of the management process. These differences are usually nothing more than a choice of words. Some consolidate similar functions into broad categories—others prefer an extensive listing of individual functions.

The management process for our purposes consists of four primary functions. These are: planning, organizing, motivating, and controlling. Good delegation, the subject of this book, requires skill in all four!

The next four pages will give you an opportunity to review your understanding of these functions.

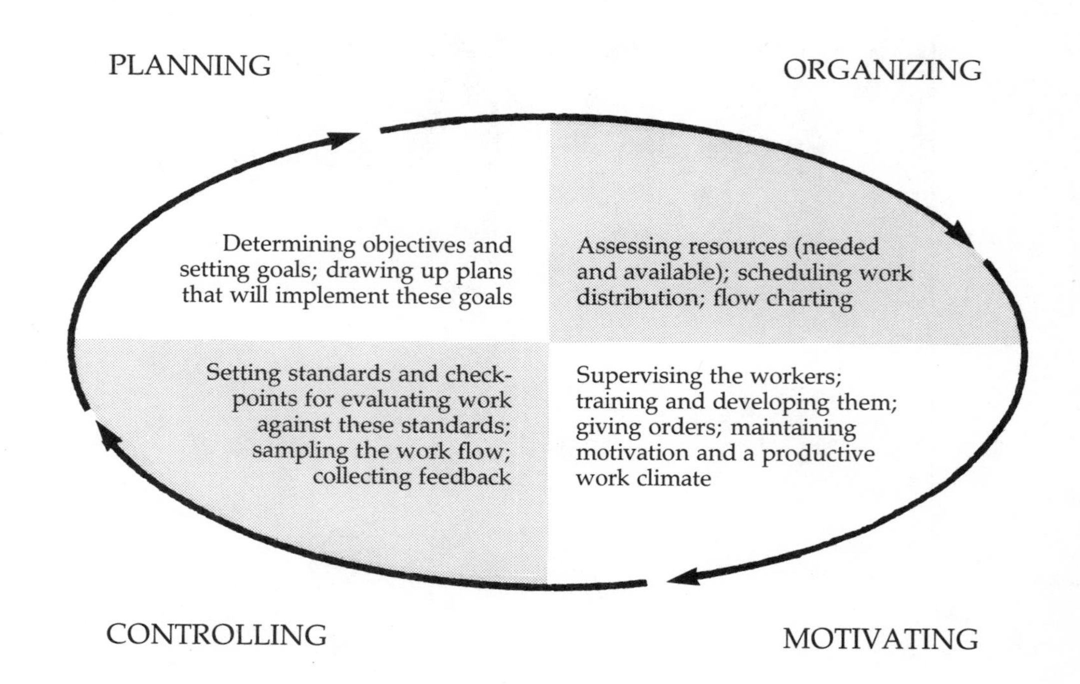

PLANNING

Planning is the thinking that precedes doing. It is concerned with setting goals and objectives for an organizational unit and with preparing plans and schedules to accomplish them. In the list below, check those statements that you consider important elements in planning.

☐ 1. Interpreting goals and objectives passed down from above as the result of planning performed at a higher level.

☐ 2. Gathering the thoughts and ideas of the employees who are directly involved, as well as your own thoughts and ideas.

☐ 3. Formulating and issuing policies and procedures to accomplish goals and objectives.

☐ 4. Examining alternatives and selecting the activities and programs that will lead to successful results.

☐ 5. Establishing timetables and completion targets in keeping with priorities.

☐ 6. Determining standards of performance and how results will be measured.

☐ 7. Identifying the resources necessary for task accomplishment—people, time, money, material—and determining their availability.

If you are an effective planner, you checked all the above.

ORGANIZING

Once planning is underway, organizing becomes essential. Resources—people, capital, equipment, raw materials, facilities—must be brought together in the most productive way to accomplish goals and objectives. In the list below, check the items that you think organizing should provide.

☐ 1. Appropriate staffing—the right number of people with the essential skills to perform the work that has to be done.

☐ 2. Delineation of responsibility and authority.

☐ 3. Alignment of major functions and structuring of the component parts into effective work units and teams.

☐ 4. Manuals, administrative guides, and other tools to make known how responsibility has been assigned and authority delegated.

☐ 5. A communications system for reporting and coordination between people and organizations.

☐ 6. Methods of problem solving and conflict resolution.

☐ 7. Facilities and equipment needed for task accomplishment.

If you checked all seven boxes, give yourself one hundred percent!

MOTIVATING

Motivation, along with planning and organizing, plays an important part in the level of performance that will be achieved in any endeavor. To check your views on motivation, review the following statements and indicate which are true and which are false.

True	False	
______	______	1. The needs and desires of employees have little bearing on motivation.
______	______	2. It is important to create an environment in which employees can meet their needs while meeting the needs of the organization.
______	______	3. Results generally improve when people are able to participate in deciding what the results should be.
______	______	4. Motivation to achieve results is improved when employees are recognized for their contributions.
______	______	5. Studies have shown that communication has very little to do with motivation.
______	______	6. Coaching and training tend to raise personal levels of motivation.
______	______	7. Motivation to achieve results usually increases as employees are given authority to make decisions affecting those results.
______	______	8. Good supervisors pay close attention to the way employees respond when they assign work.

Statements 2, 3, 4, 6, 7, and 8 are true.

CONTROLLING

Controlling is concerned with results. It involves follow-up to compare results with plans and to make adjustments where results differ from expectations. In the following list of statements about controlling, identify those you believe to be true and those you believe to be false.

Controlling requires:

True	False	
______	______	1. Devising ways to assess whether goals, objectives, or standards have been met in a timely and cost-effective manner.
______	______	2. Punishing employees who have missed their targets.
______	______	3. Formulating methods by which the use of the various resources can be measured and evaluated for future planning purposes.
______	______	4. Establishing systems that provide feedback at key points as the work progresses, so that deviations from plan can be identified, evaluated, and acted upon.
______	______	5. Limiting employee authority to minor details.
______	______	6. Reporting the status of activities and projects to those who need to know.

Statements 2 and 5 are false.

HOW WORK GETS DONE IN ORGANIZATIONS

Management is a leadership effort to integrate and effectively use a variety of resources to accomplish an objective. It applies to all organizations, whether they are businesses, hospitals, or political entities. Managers will do well to remember there is no one best way to plan, organize, motivate, or control. Each manager must continually increase his or her knowledge of management concepts and draw upon them until a winning combination is found that fits him or her, the people supervised, and the work involved.

One factor is central, however, to every management task. That factor is DELEGATION. The manager must know what is expected of his or her unit, when it is expected, and how to best employ his or her human resources to obtain the desired results. This means assigning work in a planned and thoughtful way.

> Delegation is giving people things to do. Management is accomplishing organizational goals by working through individuals and groups. It is easy to see that the two are closely entwined. And it is obvious that the manager who is not delegating is not managing.

Delegation, of all the skills and activities of a manager, is one of the most indispensable.

Case studies help provide understanding and knowledge you may not already possess. Several case problems are included in this book. Please give each your careful attention.

The first case (on the facing page) will help you understand the importance of learning and applying the concepts presented in this book.

CASE STUDY 1

The Do-It Yourself Manager

Joanne was a capable and enthusiastic professional. She was promoted to manage a group of five professionals doing work very similar to her own past assignment.

She began her new position thinking, ''I was promoted because of my excellent performance in past assignments. Therefore, I must have greater expertise than any of my subordinates and can probably do most of the work better and faster than they can. I will train them when I have time, but right now I had better concentrate on getting the work out.''

Joanne did not pass on any major assignments to her employees; she did the work herself. As time passed, her hours of work increased steadily and she was less and less available to her peers—and to her own supervisor, with whom coordination was important. Her employees were given only the most routine work, received no training, and actually knew very little about major projects in progress. One actually resigned because of the lack of challenge and personal growth. Joanne was too busy to replace him.

Finally, after sixty days, Joanne's supervisor called her in to discuss her performance. What would you have said to Joanne if you had been her supervisor? Please summarize your comments below. Then compare them with the author's on page 69.

____

____

____

TECHNICAL, HUMAN, AND CONCEPTUAL SKILLS

Many new supervisors and managers approach their jobs much like Joanne, and fall into the same trap. They do not see the difference between technical, human, and conceptual skills and how these skills apply to their position. Think of them this way.

DEFINITIONS		
Technical Skills	**Human Skills**	**Conceptual Skills**
Ability to use knowledge, methods, and equipment to perform specific tasks; acquired from experience and training.	Ability and judgment in working with people, including an understanding of motivation and leadership.	Ability to understand the complexities of the overall organization and where one's own unit fits into the total picture.

Lower-level supervisors need considerable technical skill because they are often required to train and develop new employees and technicians. At the other extreme, senior managers do not need to know how to perform all the specific tasks at the operational level, but they should understand how all the functions are interrelated. The common denominator that is crucial at all levels is human skill.

As supervisors move up in management they must learn to delegate jobs requiring technical skill to their subordinates, to give themselves time to learn the human and conceptual skills now required of them.

Top Management

Middle Management

Supervisory Management

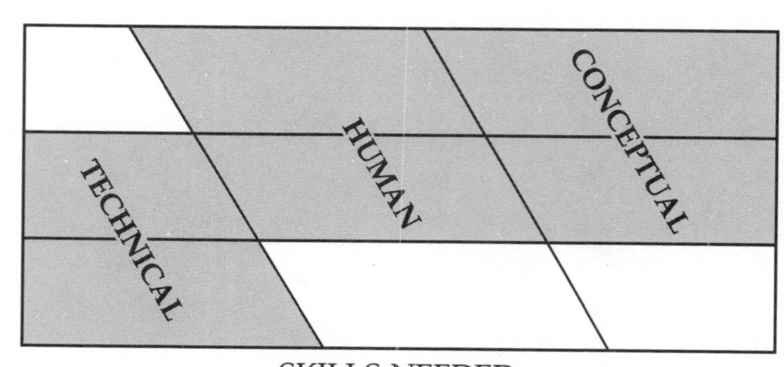

SKILLS NEEDED

WHAT CAN DELEGATING DO FOR ME?

New managers, like Joanne, often assign a low priority to delegation because they are unsure of how to go about it and don't see the benefits. Some actually think delegation is more trouble than it's worth. Some advantages of good delegation are listed below. Check those you would like to achieve.

☐ 1. More work can be accomplished and deadlines can be met more easily.

☐ 2. Employees become involved and committed.

☐ 3. The assignment of specific responsibility and authority makes control less difficult.

☐ 4. Employees grow and develop.

☐ 5. Human resources are utilized more fully and productivity improves.

☐ 6. Individual performance can be measured more accurately.

☐ 7. Compensation, including merit increases, can be more directly related to individual performance.

☐ 8. A diversity of products, operations, and people can be managed effectively.

☐ 9. Distant operations can be managed with less travel and stress.

☐ 10. Employee satisfaction and recognition are enhanced.

☐ 11. The manager has time for planning, organizing, motivating, and controlling.

☐ 12. The manager is freed to do those tasks only he or she can do.

Please add any other advantages you can think of in the spaces below.

☐ 13. ____

☐ 14. ____

☐ 15. ____

PART

II

Analyzing Personal Delegation Skills

HOW WELL DO I DELEGATE?

Here is an opportunity to learn how well you delegate. This scale will help identify your strengths and determine where improvement would be beneficial. Circle the number that best describes you. The higher the number, the more the statement describes you. When you have finished, total the numbers circled in the space provided.

Statement							
1. Each of my employees knows what I expect of her or him.	7	6	5	4	3	2	1
2. I involve employees in goal-setting, problem-solving, and productivity improvement activities.	7	6	5	4	3	2	1
3. I place my personal emphasis on planning, organizing, motivating, and controlling, rather than doing tasks others could do.	7	6	5	4	3	2	1
4. When assigning work, I select the assignee thoughtfully.	7	6	5	4	3	2	1
5. When a problem occurs on a project I have delegated, I give the employee a reasonable chance to work it out for him/herself.	7	6	5	4	3	2	1
6. When I delegate work to employees, I brief them fully on the details with which I am familiar.	7	6	5	4	3	2	1
7. I see delegation as one way to help employees develop their skills, and I assign work accordingly.	7	6	5	4	3	2	1
8. I support and help employees in emergencies, but I do not permit them to leave work for me to do.	7	6	5	4	3	2	1
9. When I assign work, I stress the results desired, not how to accomplish them.	7	6	5	4	3	2	1
10. When I delegate a project, I make sure everyone concerned knows who is in charge.	7	6	5	4	3	2	1
11. When delegating work, I balance authority with need and experience.	7	6	5	4	3	2	1
12. I hold my employees responsible for results.	7	6	5	4	3	2	1

TOTAL ________

A score between 72 and 84 suggests you are on target. A score between 48 and 71 indicates you are getting by, but could improve. Anything below 48 means you need to make changes.

SYMPTOMS OF POOR DELEGATION

There are many symptoms of poor delegation. They can usually be seen in the work habits of the manager, the attitude of the employees, or the productivity of the group. In the list below, check the symptoms that are visible in your organization.

- ☐ Deadlines are frequently missed.
- ☐ Some employees are much busier than others.
- ☐ The supervisor (me) is usually too busy to talk to employees.
- ☐ Employees are unsure of their authority.
- ☐ No one in the unit is ever ready for promotion.
- ☐ Employee decisions are often overruled.
- ☐ No one seems to know who is in charge of a project.
- ☐ The organization is plagued by slow decision making.
- ☐ The supervisor (me) never has time to visit employee work areas.
- ☐ Changes in plans and objectives are not passed on to employees with a need to know.
- ☐ Employees are assigned tasks they can't handle without training.
- ☐ The supervisor (me) sometimes intervenes in a project or assignment without informing the delegatee.
- ☐ Employees frequently request transfers to other units.
- ☐ The communications flow is sporadic, incomplete, and often too late.
- ☐ The supervisor (me) often takes work home and sometimes reschedules his or her vacation because of the work load.
- ☐ Talented employees are bored.
- ☐ The supervisor (me) insists all mail must first pass through his or her office.

If you checked more than one or two of the above statements, you should look carefully at your delegation practices and ask yourself why these conditions exist.

COMMON BARRIERS TO DELEGATION

Ineffective delegators rationalize their inadequacies in various ways. They usually center around obstacles (natural or self-made) in themselves, in the characteristics of their employees, or in the situation itself. In the following list of attitudes, indicate those that affect your delegation practices by checking Yes. If they do not affect you, check No. Think about each statement carefully and be totally honest.

Yes	No	SELF-IMPOSED OBSTACLES
______	______	I prefer performing operating tasks—not management functions—because I understand them better and I know how.
______	______	I can do the work in my unit better than anyone else.
______	______	I don't know how to delegate.
______	______	My employees won't like me if I expect too much of them.
______	______	I am not certain to whom I should delegate.
______	______	It is easier and quicker to do things myself.
______	______	We just can't afford to make any mistakes.
		EMPLOYEE-IMPOSED OBSTACLES
______	______	My employees lack experience and competence.
______	______	My employees are already overloaded.
______	______	My employees resist responsibility.
______	______	My employees fear criticism and avoid risk.
		SITUATION-IMPOSED OBSTACLES
______	______	Management expects me to handle the really important tasks personally.
______	______	My employees can't be trusted to work on their own.
______	______	We are seriously understaffed. I have no one to whom I can delegate.
______	______	Most of our decisions are made under crisis conditions.

If you answered yes to any of the above, you will find this book most helpful.

FACT VERSUS FANCY

The statements on the preceding page that you answered ''yes'' need to be examined objectively. They usually are invalid and keep supervisors from delegating as they should. Several of them deserve close scrutiny.

The Fallacy of Omnipotence

This is the ''I can do it better myself'' syndrome. Even if it is true, the choice is not between the quality of the supervisor's work on a given task and that of the employee. The choice is between the benefits of the supervisor's performance on a single task versus the benefits of spending his or her time in planning, organizing, motivating, controlling, and developing an effective team. The team will eventually outperform the manager and continue to grow.

The Fear of Being Disliked

Though few managers will admit it, most are concerned that their employees will dislike or resent them if they press them with a lot of work. Such a manager will risk personal burnout rather than inconvenience an employee.

Interestingly enough, employees rate supervisors who make full use of delegation good or excellent. Poor delegators receive low ratings.

Lack of Confidence in Employees

Managers who lack confidence in their employees should look to themselves for the answer. They are, or should be, in control of the situation.

If employees cannot handle delegated assignments, the manager has either hired incompetent people, failed to provide them with appropriate training, or has not made the effort to find out the extent of their capabilities. The remedy: identify strengths and weaknesses, and train or replace those who still cannot meet standards.

Employees Expect the Answers from Me

This is usually how managers rationalize taking problem solving and decision making away from employees. It occurs when an employee brings a problem to a supervisor who says, "Why don't you leave it with me and I'll get back to you." When the supervisor does get back to the employee it is with the solution. The employee only wanted to talk about the problem—she didn't want the answer.

I Can Do It Faster Than I Can Explain It

A supervisor who uses this excuse to justify doing an operating task that he or she likes to do but someone else could be taught to do, is making a serious mistake. If he or she doesn't take the time to teach someone else the task, he or she will still be performing it far into the future. This consumes valuable time and effort that could be better spent on tasks only the supervisor can do.

Sometimes a supervisor truly cannot delegate. But as the chart below demonstrates, upward progression requires more and more delegating and less "doing."

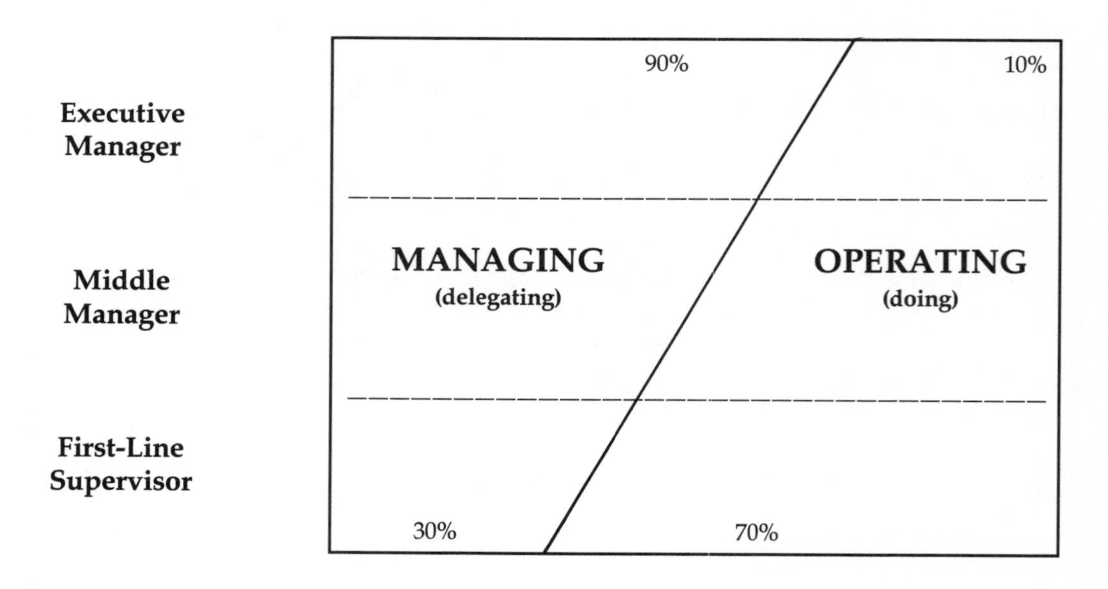

PART

III

Preparing to Delegate

ANALYZE YOUR JOB

To become an effective delegator, you must have your own job well in hand. This means periodically:

- Reviewing your duties and responsibilities as a manager. How have they changed? What new things do you have to learn? How do they affect your unit? What are the new challenges? What old practices need to be stopped?
- Reaffirming the primary objectives of your unit. Have there been any changes that affect priorities or need to be communicated to employees?
- Highlighting the key results areas. What are the make or break factors in your assignment? What are the areas in which specific results are essential?
- Reexamining your work load to identify those few tasks only you can do.

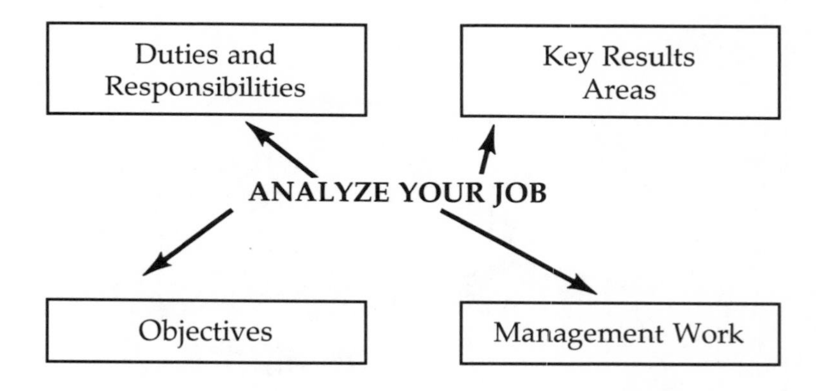

Remember, you are a manager, not an individual contributor. It is your job to utilize your human resources effectively to accomplish organizational goals. You must sort out the important from the unimportant and proceed on a priority basis. The more you develop your people, and the more you delegate to them, the more they can help you identify key results areas and meet objectives. Let go of tasks that rightfully belong to your employees. That includes trouble shooting and problem solving in their areas of responsibility. Be sure they are properly trained and help them when they flounder, but by all means give them a chance to do the job for which they were hired.

DECIDE WHAT TO DELEGATE

ANY TIME YOU PERFORM A TASK SOMEONE ELSE COULD DO, YOU KEEP YOURSELF FROM A TASK ONLY YOU CAN DO.

Managers usually delegate to give themselves more time to do complex and difficult management tasks, to improve productivity, or to develop their employees. Some types of work you should consider delegating are listed below.

DECISIONS YOU MAKE MOST FREQUENTLY.

Minor decisions and repetitive routines often consume a major portion of the day. Most, if not all, of these can be delegated by teaching employees the policies and procedures that apply. They probably already know the details better than you.

List two possibilities:

1. ______________________________

2. ______________________________

FUNCTIONS THAT ARE IN YOUR TECHNICAL OR FUNCTIONAL SPECIALTY.

These are usually operating tasks rather than management functions. You can teach others to do them. In fact, your challenge as a manager is to motivate others to produce better results than you ever did as an individual performer. Part of the time you save can be used to learn about other functions you supervise, so you can manage them better.

List two possibilities:

1. ______________________________

2. ______________________________

TASKS AND PROJECTS FOR WHICH YOU ARE LEAST QUALIFIED.

It is almost certain that some of your employees are better qualified and can do parts of the job better than you. Let them.

List two possibilities:

1. ______________________________

2. ______________________________

FUNCTIONS YOU DISLIKE.

Performing functions we dislike is distasteful, and we often put them off or do them poorly. Examine the likes and dislikes of your staff as well as their talents. You will nearly always find someone who likes the job and can do it well. If they need training, provide it.

List two possibilities:

1. ______________________________

2. ______________________________

WORK THAT WILL PROVIDE EXPERIENCE FOR EMPLOYEES.

This makes growth in the present job a reality and helps keep employees challenged and motivated.

List two possibilities:

1. ______________________________

2. ______________________________

ASSIGNMENTS THAT WILL ADD VARIETY TO ROUTINE WORK.

A change of pace is usually welcome and is often a good motivator for an employee whose job is growing dull.

List two possibilities:

1. ______________________________

2. ______________________________

ACTIVITIES THAT WILL MAKE A POSITION MORE COMPLETE.

As employees become more proficient, they often have time to spare. Add complementary duties and responsibilities to give their positions more substance.

List two possibilities:

1. ______________________________

2. ______________________________

TASKS THAT WILL INCREASE THE NUMBER OF PEOPLE WHO CAN PERFORM CRITICAL ASSIGNMENTS.

Maximize the strength of the group by giving people the needed experience to back one another up during emergencies or periods of unusually heavy work.

List two possibilities:

1. ______________________________

2. ______________________________

OPPORTUNITIES TO USE AND REINFORCE CREATIVE TALENTS.

Employees are not creative in a stifling environment. Stimulate them with difficult problems and projects, and reward creative solutions.

List two possibilities:

1. ______________________________

2. ______________________________

TARGETED DELEGATION

BAFFLED BY THE BUDGET

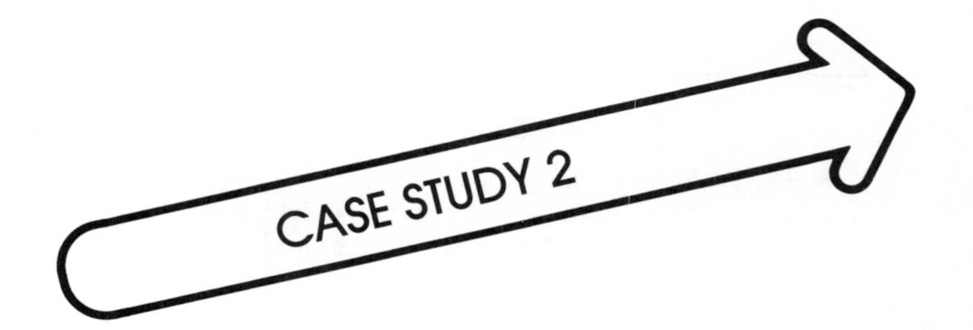

CASE STUDY 2

Baffled by the Budget

Jack is an excellent manager of manufacturing, but he just learned in a performance review that he may have a fatal flaw. He is always over budget and his explanations are usually weak and late. This happens even though he prepares the budget himself, and personally maintains what appear to be adequate controls. Now his supervisor has given him an ultimatum: ''Get control of your budget or I will have to demote you to a less responsible position.''

Jack's administrative assistant, who has an excellent accounting background, expertise with computers, and some experience with budgets, would like to help. So would his section heads, who believe the budget would be more representative of reality if they had some input. Jack, however, feels it is his responsibility and he has to do it himself.

In the space below, outline what you would suggest that Jack do to correct this obviously serious problem. Then check your answer with the author's suggestions on page 69.

MY SUGGESTIONS:

____

____

____

____

____

____

____

____

____

____

____

TASK/PROJECT

Key Results Areas	Results Expected	Critical Time Lines

This planning sheet, plus the checklist on page 28 will help you more effectively plan your next delegation.

ANALYSIS PLANNING SHEET

Standards to Be Met	Budget	Critical Interfaces	Frequency of Feedback

PLANNING THE DELEGATION

Deciding what to delegate is only the first step in the delegation process. Delegation, like most other management tasks, is most successful when it's planned. It may take a few minutes, for simple tasks; or a few hours, when the project is complex. Your planning should include at least the following considerations. In the checklist below, check *Yes* if you include the item in your planning; check *No* if you do not.

Yes	No	
______	______	1. What is the objective to be accomplished?
______	______	2. What are the critical completion dates?
______	______	3. What standards will have to be met?
______	______	4. What decisions will have to be made?
______	______	5. How much authority can I delegate?
______	______	6. How much authority will I delegate?
______	______	7. What instructions or orders will the person(s) be authorized to issue?
______	______	8. Does a budget need to be developed or followed?
______	______	9. Who will the person(s) need to interface with in my unit. In other units?
______	______	10. What information do I need to give?
______	______	11. How much do I want to be involved?
______	______	12. What feedback do I want and when do I want it?
______	______	13. Who will I need to keep informed of progress?
______	______	14. Do I need to tell others who is in charge?
______	______	15. To whom should I delegate?

If you check No for any of the above items, plan on changing your delegation behavior so that you can check them Yes in the future.

P A R T

IV

Selecting the Right Person

MAKING CHOICES

As soon as you have completed your delegation plan, identify the appropriate person to perform the task. Some of the many things to consider are listed below.

DOES THE WORK BELONG TO A PARTICULAR POSITION?

Some tasks or projects fit right into existing work assignments and can be logically delegated there.

List two examples from the past or two possibilities for the future:

1. ______________________________

2. ______________________________

WHO HAS THE INTEREST AND/OR THE ABILITY?

Analyze employee job performance periodically, and keep an inventory of the interests and abilities of your staff. Look for opportunities to give employees who are attending classes a chance to apply what they are learning.

Give consideration to interest as well as ability. A minimally qualified person may take the assignment enthusiastically and develop the required skills; the best-qualified person with a low level of interest may do a poor job.

List two examples from the past or two prospects for the future:

1. ______________________________

2. ______________________________

WHO WILL FIND THE WORK CHALLENGING?

Studies reflect that large numbers of employees are unchallenged, and their boredom is reflected in their performance. Give them the pleasure of a new opportunity to achieve.

List two prospects for the future:

1. ______________________________

2. ______________________________

WHO WILL THE ASSIGNMENT STRETCH AND HELP TO GROW?

Some employees thrive on challenge and are willing to develop new skills to meet new job requirements. Give them the opportunity.

Identify two people in this category:

1. ______________________________

2. ______________________________

WHO HAS BEEN OVERLOOKED WHEN YOU HAVE DELEGATED IN THE PAST?

Delegate to all of your employees and stretch them when you can. Avoid playing favorites or overburdening some of your staff.

Delegating to an employee who has been untested in the past requires careful planning, but the payoff in added performance is potentially high.

An assignment delegated with care can bring a problem employee up to standard. An employee with unused potential can be motivated to new heights of achievement.

Every time you give an ''unknown'' the chance to perform in a new way, the overall depth, versatility, and morale of your unit will improve.

List two possibilities for the future:

1. ______________________________

2. ______________________________

WHO HAS THE TIME?

If an employee has occasional periods with a light work load, look for opportunities to productively use that employee's time.

List two possibilities:

1. ______________________________

2. ______________________________

WHO IS BEING PREPARED FOR A NEW ASSIGNMENT OR PROMOTION?

Employees being prepared for a new assignment or promotion often profit from delegated assignments that relate to their new duties and responsibilities.

List two possibilities:

1. ______________________________

2. ______________________________

YOU REALLY DON'T KNOW WHAT PEOPLE CAN DO UNTIL YOU GIVE THEM A CHANCE UNDER THE PROPER CONDITIONS.

MAKING THE PREDELEGATION ASSESSMENT

The planning phase prior to assigning work is the manager's opportunity to organize the distribution of work and to schedule it within his or her unit. The quality of your preparations will largely determine the success of the delegation. Managers who ignore the planning are usually those who are keeping far too much work to themselves, or those who indiscriminately dump assignments on staff members. Asking yourself the following questions in advance will help you make better delegation decisions:

1. What work needs to be done?
2. What can and should be delegated?
3. What is the best match of work with individual employee abilities and interests?
4. Who would the assignment help develop?
5. Who can do it for me now?
6. Who can be trained to do it?
7. What is the employee's current work load and level of performance?
8. What is my best course of action, other than doing it myself, given the time contraints involved?

The chart on the next page is a good place to summarize an record your thoughts.

DELEGATION

Key Results Areas	Results Expected	Who Can Do It for Me Now

LOG

Who Can Be Trained to Do It	Assigned To	Follow-Up Required

REMEMBER YOUR SECRETARY'S POTENTIAL

Managers with secretaries, or administrative assistants, often fail to delegate properly to them. They see them only as someone to do word processing, answer the telephones, and keep up the files. This is a major mistake.

When secretaries have been properly trained and participate actively in the management of their supervisor's business affairs, they can be of incalculable value in a number of areas. Consider the following possibilities. As you do, check the tasks you already delegate to your secretary or admininistrative assistant, and be alert to new ways to enrich their jobs and facilitate your own.

☐ 1. Screening and directing mail to the proper person for action.

☐ 2. Composing correspondence for your signature.

☐ 3. Organizing your time, coordinating appointments, and assuring deadlines are met.

☐ 4. Following up on reports and other work on which you, or others, have set a due date, and reporting their status to you.

☐ 5. Coordinating conference calls.

☐ 6. Organizing and setting up meetings on your behalf.

☐ 7. Gathering information needed for decision making.

☐ 8. Maintaining appropriate personal records and files.

☐ 9. Redirecting telephone calls and correspondence that come to you, but should go elsewhere.

☐ 10. Performing basic research on projects you have retained for yourself.

☐ 11. Maintaining confidential records.

☐ 12. Facilitating communication through your office in your absence.

Add other possibilities that fit your situation:

☐ 13. ____

☐ 14. ____

☐ 15. ____

CASE 3

CASE STUDY 3

Making Choices

Susan has been in her new managerial assignment for approximately two months. She is trying to make the transition from being an outstanding individual performer to an effective manager. Delegation is very difficult for her, but she is making a real effort to learn to do it well. She directs a group of eight.

Her supervisor asked her recently how she was doing with her delegation efforts. Susan replied, ''I think I am doing pretty well. I have learned that Mary Wong is very knowledgeable about all aspects of the work, and she always completes the assignments I give her on time—even if she has to work overtime and on the weekends. So I give her all the big jobs and let the others stick to the routines they know best. My other employees just aren't qualified to carry the burden that Mary does.''

If you were Mary's supervisor, how would you respond?

____

____

____

____

____

____

____

____

____

____

____

____

Check your answer with the author's on page 70.

PART

V

Making the Delegation

COMMUNICATING THE DELEGATION

> The heart of the delegation process is the interaction between the supervisor and the employee when the assignment is made.

This face-to-face, two-way discussion is the critical step that should end with employee commitment and the supervisor's assurance that the results needed will be achieved.

Delegation is not just pushing work down. When you are delegating, you are consulting and developing as well as assigning work. Open communication is vital, and success depends ultimately on the communication skills of the manager and the employee and on the quality of their relationship. When there is a lack of trust on either side, or poor communication between them, the needed understanding and motivation is unlikely to be there.

The following steps are essential in communicating an assignment:

1. DESCRIBE AS FULLY AS POSSIBLE THE PROJECT OR TASK AND THE RESULTS EXPECTED.

   Pass on all the information needed to get the job started, or let the employee know where it can be obtained. Indicate who else will be involved and describe their roles.

2. AGREE ON STANDARDS OF PERFORMANCE AND TIMETABLES.

   The scope of the assignment has already been determined, but you will want the employee's input on standards and a reasonable timetable for completion of the assignment.

3. DETERMINE ANY TRAINING OR SPECIAL HELP THAT WILL BE NEEDED, AND WHEN IT WILL BE PROVIDED.

4. DEFINE PARAMETERS AND THE RESOURCES, INCLUDING BUDGET, THAT WILL BE AVAILABLE.

5. STATE THE AMOUNT AND FREQUENCY OF FEEDBACK YOU EXPECT.

6. SPELL OUT THE AMOUNT OF AUTHORITY BEING DELEGATED.

   This should be balanced according to the complexity of the task, your confidence in the employee, and your need to keep others informed.

   See page 43 for selection of an appropriate level.

7. TELL OTHERS WHO IS IN CHARGE.

   It is important you do not become a communications block between the delegatee and others who will be involved or affected.

> It is easy to see from these seven basic points that delegation is *not* more trouble than it's worth. Have you been missing some good opportunities because you thought it was?

MISSED OPPORTUNITIES

Supervisors who find themselves deeply involved in the detailed work of their units sometimes wake up to the fact that the job is controlling them. They are controlling nothing. If they examine the situation carefully (while pondering the fact that their employees went home hours ago and they are still working), they often see the reason for their plight. Their reaction is usually, ''If I had delegated this to Clifford or Sue in the first place, I wouldn't be having this problem now.''

How many times have you missed the opportunity to delegate, or thought you had, and found yourself doing work someone else could and should have done?

By now, some missed opportunities to delegate have no doubt come to mind. List them in the space provided below. . . and resolve not to let it happen again.

MY MISSED OPPORTUNITIES

SIX LEVELS OF AUTHORITY

A common management mistake is failing to delegate the right amount of authority considering the task, the surrounding circumstances, and the employee's ability. Some managers do not delegate any authority because they want full personal control. Others give full authority because they want to be free of the task. Most of the time, something in between these two extremes is called for. Before you make your next delegation, review the authority levels described on the next page and select one that fits your needs.

THE DO-IT-YOURSELF MANAGER
WHO HATES TO GIVE UP CONTROL

SIX LEVELS OF AUTHORITY

Level of Authority	Assignment	Reason
1	Look into the situation. Get all the facts and report them to me. I'll decide what to do.	The employee is new to the job and the supervisor wants to retain control of the outcome.
2	Identify the problem. Determine alternative solutions and the pluses and minuses of each. Recommend one for my approval.	The employee is being developed and the supervisor wants to see how he or she approaches problems and makes decisions.
3	Examine the issues. Let me know what you intend to do, but don't take action until you check with me.	The supervisor has confidence in the employee, but does not want action taken without his or her approval. This may be because of constraints from higher management, or the need to communicate the action to others before it is taken.

Level of Authority	Assignment	Reason
4	Solve the problem. Let me know what you intend to do, then do it, unless I say no.	The supervisor has respect for the employee's ability and judgment, and only wants a final check before action is taken.
5	Take action on this matter, and let me know what you did.	The supervisor has full confidence in the employee and has no need to be consulted before action is taken. He or she wants to know the outcome.
6	Take action. No further contact with me is necessary.	The supervisor has total confidence in the employee. The employee has full authority to act and does not need to report the results back to the supervisor.

FOLLOWING THROUGH

> The goal in delegation is satisfactory completion of the assigned task or project through the personal efforts of those handling tasks.

It is important, however, that the manager follow through with any support, resources, or information promised. It is also important that a feedback mechanism, suitable to the situation, be established between the employee assigned and the manager. These considerations are all part of the preparations for delegation, and should be covered when the delegation is made.

THE ESSENTIAL ELEMENTS OF FOLLOW-THROUGH		
The Manager's Role	The Manager's Communication	The Manager's Action
Encourage independence. Allow freedom of action in keeping with the level of delegation. Support initiative and creativity. Share opinions and show interest. Accept mistakes and learn from them. Provide training when needed. Live with differences as long as objectives are met. Be available. Don't take the job back unless absolutely essential (coach through problems).	Share all pertinent information. Do not become a communications block between the employee and the others involved. Monitor progress, but do not hover. Provide honest feedback. Insist that your need to know be fulfilled on time.	Assess results. Suggest course corrections if appropriate and unrecognized by the those handling tasks. Help solve problems, but only those beyond the employee's ability to handle. Evaluate performance. Plan any needed training for the future. Compliment efforts and reward success.

CASE STUDY 4

The Incomplete Data Dilemma

Marla is the manager of an insurance company claims group. Her employees are well trained and have considerable experience in claims work. Much of the work is routine, but occasionally an unusual claim is submitted that requires a great deal of investigation. When this occurs, Marla assigns one of her claims representatives to the case. She delegates the authority necessary for that person to gather the facts, develop alternative solutions, and recommend the action to be taken. However, something always seems to go wrong. Key information is lacking or has not been considered. This is true even though Marla often acts as the point of contact when people outside the company are providing pertinent data. She always tries to pass this information on quickly and in a form the those handling the assignment will understand.

She has had several discussions with her staff about this, but the discussions only make them angry and defensive.

What do you think the problem is? Jot down your ideas in the space below.

____

____

____

____

____

____

____

____

Turn to page 70 and check your ideas with those of the author.

PART

VI

Preparing Employees for Delegation

WHAT YOU SHOULD EXPECT

The manager has every right to expect results from the employee according to the parameters established when the delegation was made. Check the expectations you feel are currently being satisfied when you delegate:

☐ 1. The employee has a willing, can-do attitude and accepts responsibility for the task.

☐ 2. The employee asks questions and seeks help when needed.

☐ 3. Progress reports are furnished on time to you and to others in the communications loop.

☐ 4. The finished tasks are good examples of completed staff work.

☐ 5. The employee uses initiative and shows dedication and commitment to the task.

☐ 6. Time, money, equipment, and manpower are seen as expensive resources and used accordingly.

> If these expectations are to be met, the employee must be prepared in advance, permitted to grow as the work is done, and continuously developed for heavier assignments in the future.

PREPARATION BEGINS WITH EMPLOYMENT

If a manager is to have a strong team to whom he or she can delegate, they must be hired with that thought in mind. Human resources are the most critical part of any manager's success. Good people help insure profitability, productivity, growth, and long-term survival. Some critical elements in employee selection and placement are listed below. Indicate how well you perform by checking the appropriate box.

	Do Well	Should Improve
1. I analyze job requirements thoroughly before beginning the selection process.	☐	☐
2. I always probe for objective evidence of a candidate's skills; knowledge; past successes and failures; dependability; and attitude toward work, coworkers, supervisors, and customers.	☐	☐
3. I determine the type of project and task responsibility the applicant has had in previous positions, and how they have handled authority.	☐	☐
4. I make sure each applicant understands the job requirements and expected standards of performance.	☐	☐
5. I describe my idea of teamwork to applicants and ask them to assess how they would work under team conditions.	☐	☐
6. In making a selection decision, I evaluate facts carefully and avoid making premature conclusions or stereotyping.	☐	☐
7. People I hire are placed in positions where there is potential for success.	☐	☐

> If the people you select to be on your team are successful, you will be successful.

DEVELOP EMPLOYEES TO HANDLE COMPLEX TASKS

Do you use delegation to build new employee skills and strengthen existing ones? Do you prepare people properly for assignments you wish to delegate to them? Your attitude, knowledge, and approach will influence what is learned and how well it is applied. Here are some suggestions to improve the return on investment in training for all concerned.

Place a ✓ check in the box if you already do what is suggested. Place an X in the box if you plan to begin this practice.

I normally:

☐ 1. Review performance against expectations with each employee, and jointly identify training that will strengthen results.

☐ 2. Listen to employees' growth objectives and support them through delegation when I can.

☐ 3. Talk in advance to employees selected for training, to emphasize the importance of the training to their job and their delegated assignments.

☐ 4. Have an employee's work covered by others while that employee is in formal training, so he or she can concentrate on what is being taught.

☐ 5. Help employees develop an action plan to apply their training to the job and to any additional assignments I delegate.

☐ 6. Ask the employees for an evaluation of the training program and whether it would be suitable for other members of the team.

☐ 7. Delegate work to employees that allows them to apply new techniques and methods learned during training.

☐ 8. Compliment employees when they apply their newly acquired skills.

> Qualified employees are receptive to delegation and the growth opportunities it provides.

TEACH EMPLOYEES PROBLEM-SOLVING TECHNIQUES

Many supervisors spend too much time solving problems that could be better handled by the employees they supervise. When supervisors try to solve all the problems, production is slowed, employees are frustrated, and personal growth is limited. The supervisor ends up with less time to plan, organize, motivate, and control. Delegation is more effective when the supervisor participates in problem solving only when necessary, instead of dominating it. In view of this, problem solving should be taught at every level of the organization.

The problem solving process should be as simple as possible while getting the job done. One basic approach is outlined below. Check those steps that would be useful in your operation:

☐ **STEP 1—State what appears to be the problem.**
The real problem may not surface until facts have been gathered and analyzed. Therefore, start with a supposition that can later be confirmed or corrected.

☐ **STEP 2—Gather facts, feelings, and opinions.**
What happened? Where, when, and how did it occur? What is its size, scope, and severity? Who and what is affected? Is it likely to happen again? Does it need to be corrected? Time and expense may require problem solvers to think through what they need, and assign priorities to the more critical elements.

☐ **STEP 3—Restate the problem.**
The facts help make this possible, and provide supporting data. The actual problem may or may not be the same as stated in Step 1.

☐ **STEP 4—Identify alternative solutions.**
Generate ideas. Do not eliminate any possible solutions until several have been discussed.

☐ **STEP 5—Evaluate alternatives.**
Which will provide the optimum solution? What are the risks? Are the costs in keeping with the benefits? Will the solution create new problems?

☐ **STEP 6—Implement the decision.**
Who must be involved? To what extent? How, when, and where? Who will the decision impact? What might go wrong? How will results be reported and verified?

☐ **STEP 7—Evaluate the results.**
Test the solution against the desired results. Modify the solution if better results are needed.

MAKE EMPLOYEE COMMITMENT POSSIBLE

Managers cannot do it all, no matter how talented and committed they may be. Their success is measured by their ability to delegate intelligently and then motivate employees to accomplish the goals of the organization. The highest level of achievement is attained when a team is committed to the task and full use is made of each member's talents.

Commitment cannot be forced. It is self-generating and usually develops through a feeling of involvement. People increase commitment to a team when they are allowed to contribute to its success. Once a person is actively involved in delegated projects and activities, including problem solving, a sense of ownership is developed. People feel more important and needed when they share a responsibility for results. Employees contribute their best to problem solving when they have a personal stake in doing so.

A manager controls the degree to which employees are involved. Open up opportunities for participation through delegation, and watch the commitment grow.

DIFFERENCES BETWEEN DELEGATORS

The manager's attitude toward employees and their ability to handle delegated assignments can make a significant difference. In the two lists below, check those items that best describe you.

Success-Centered Delegator	Doubt-Centered Delegator
☐ Concentrates on successful results and high goals.	☐ Focuses on and transmits fear of failure. Sets fail-safe goals.
☐ Reinforces employee's strengths and abilities. Confident of success.	☐ Expresses grave doubts about the employee's ability and limits, or reduces authority arbitrarily.
☐ Encourages employee participation in setting goals and objectives.	☐ Personally sets arbitrary goals and objectives.
☐ Readily accepts new ideas and creative solutions.	☐ Discourages anything new or untried.
☐ Communicates freely and openly. Nothing is held back.	☐ Withholds information to force the employee to ask for help.
☐ Recognizes achievement and reinforces it.	☐ Doesn't recognize success until it is endorsed from above.
☐ Looks at the implications of each assignment for the future and assigns tasks accordingly.	☐ Focuses on short-range goals and discourages employees who see implications for the future.
☐ Encourages employees to appraise their performance and suggest improvements.	☐ Tells people what went wrong and what to do about it.

CASE STUDY 5

The Delegation Disaster

When Jim took over the systems group in the Electronics Division, he made up his mind to change the environment and hopefully the attitudes of the employees. His predecessor had not been an effective delegator or communicator. The employees had little to do in a department where the supervisor was totally swamped.

Jim immediately began to delegate assignments (at fairly high authority levels) that his predecessor had performed herself. He was surprised at the results.

His employees seemed to think he was pushing *his* work on them. Most of them complained they were neither trained nor paid to do the assignments delegated. It was not unusual for them to bring problems arising from their normal assignments to Jim for solutions, and they did not understand him saying, ''Don't bring me problems, bring me solutions.''

Has Jim overlooked anything in his approach to turning this situation around? Make your comments in the space below.

____

____

____

____

____

____

____

____

____

See page 71 for the author's comments.

P A R T

VII

Potential Delegation Problems and How to Handle Them

DELEGATOR'S TROUBLE-SHOOTING GUIDE

Possible Problems	Possible Solutions
1. Supervisor delegates only meaningless chores.	Delegating only meaningless chores creates resentment. Mix in some of your favorite things and share the good times.
2. Employees resist the work, claiming they don't know how to do it.	Provide training as necessary, or break down the job and let them handle as many components as they can. Add more as they learn.
3. The employee says he or she is too busy.	If that is true, consider giving the task to someone else, but verify their work load first.
4. The task is repetitive, but it would take you longer to delegate the job than to do it yourself.	Get smart. At least have someone start to learn the process. Soon they will be doing it all. Otherwise you will still be doing it next year.
5. "Higher management requires me to sign these invoices and other basic documents like shipping and receiving papers."	Ask management to change the policy so employees closer to the work can sign. You're probably already taking their word that it's all right to do so.
6. "Poor results on this project will make me look bad."	Your job is to let subordinates develop by taking on new endeavors. They may make some mistakes, but they will learn from them. You can minimize serious mistakes by using an appropriate level of delegation.
7. "If my employees can do the tough jobs well, I'm not needed."	Management desperately needs managers who can get superior performance from employees. Keep up the good work!

TROUBLE-SHOOTING GUIDE (Continued)

Possible Problems	Possible Solutions
8. ''My supervisor expects me to do this personally.''	If that is the actual case, you had better do it, but first check it out with the boss. She or he may just want to be sure you see that it gets done.
9. ''I'll lose my skills if I delegate too much of the work.''	Managers need to learn to manage. They need to teach their employees the skills needed for what they used to do.
10. ''If I delegate all my work, I won't have anything to do.''	Direct your attention to planning, organizing, motivating, and controlling.
11. ''I don't understand the work well enough to control it or make a judgment about how well it is being done.''	Learn enough about unfamiliar areas to ask the right questions and assess the answers.
12. Employees with delegated tasks keep coming back for advice and help.	Whenever an employee asks how you would do the task, turn it around and ask how she or he would do it. Reinforce correct answers warmly. If you feel sure she or he can handle the problem, or the consequences of an error are low, be unavailable. Help them build confidence.
13. Some employees are overburdened and others don't have enough to do.	The supervisor is overdelegating to those who are most trusted, and failing to develop those in whom she or he lacks confidence. It is essential to balance the work and raise the confidence level by giving everyone a chance to perform.

TROUBLE-SHOOTING GUIDE (Continued)

Possible Problems	Possible Solutions
14. Employees do not understand organizational objectives and standards.	Tell the employees what is at stake and the why of the job. As often as you can, involve the employees in setting objectives and standards.
15. ''Employees don't do things the way I do.''	Concentrate on getting the right results and learn to live with differences. You may even learn something new.
16. The supervisor either delegates everything or nothing.	Study the levels of delegation described on page 44 and learn to apply them.
17. The supervisor assigns the least challenging work to the most qualified people.	Sometimes necessary, but often done because the supervisor fears mistakes. Select a level of delegation that fits the employee and the situation. Some mistakes will occur; they will provide learning experiences. It's a serious mistake to burn out your best people.
18. The supervisor and the employee have trouble agreeing on the specifics of the delegation.	Review and clarify objectives, to be sure they are understood. Delegate accordingly. Don't be a nitpicker. Follow up as necessary to see that the right results are being obtained.
19. The employee's performance is jeopardizing a successful outcome.	Identify the reason and take corrective action. This might include changing the level of authority and providing more support. Acting carelessly could shatter the employee's confidence.
20. Deadlines are not being met.	Reassess objectives, standards, and priorities with the employee. Identify the reasons for missed deadlines and take corrective action.

P A R T

VIII

Review and Commitment to the Future

CONGRATULATIONS!

You have completed the activities and exercises in this book. It's time now to measure your progress. Which of the statements on the facing page are true and which are false?

REVIEW

Answer the following true/false questions.

True	False	
______	______	1. Most managers excel at delegation.
______	______	2. Delegation is an indispensable management skill.
______	______	3. It's all right to delegate tasks you dislike.
______	______	4. Delegation is essential to the development of employees and the improvement of productivity.
______	______	5. Employees appreciate your intervention in their decision making.
______	______	6. The list of tasks a manager cannot delegate is quite long.
______	______	7. Employees dislike managers who delegate.
______	______	8. As you move up, you must learn to delegate operating tasks you once performed yourself.
______	______	9. Delegation is one way to use and reinforce creative talents.
______	______	10. Managers must always keep key results areas in mind when delegating.
______	______	11. Delegation is a positive act and requires very little thought or preparation.
______	______	12. You don't really know what people can do until you give them a chance under the proper conditions.
______	______	13. Secretaries should be restricted to word processing, filing, and answering phones.
______	______	14. The heart of the delegation process is the interaction between the supervisor and employee when the assignment is communicated.
______	______	15. A common management mistake is failing to delegate authority commensurate with the task.
______	______	16. The goal in delegation is the satisfactory completion of the assigned task through the personal efforts of those assigned the task.
______	______	17. Teaching employees to solve problems helps prepare them for delegation.
______	______	18. Any time you perform a task someone else could do, you keep yourself from a task only you can do.

Check your answers with the author's on the next page.

REVIEW ANSWERS

1. False. Name five in your circle of acquaintances.
2. True. If you are not delegating, you are not managing.
3. True. Chances are very good you will find someone who enjoys them. We usually don't do very well what we dislike.
4. True. Try it, you'll like the results.
5. False. Do you like it?
6. False. Make a list. You will be amazed how short it is (if you are honest).
7. False. Research reflects just the opposite.
8. True. If you don't, your upward progress will stop or you will burn out.
9. True. If you don't delegate, creativity will die.
10. True. Accomplishing results in key results areas is what your job is all about.
11. False. Thought and preparation assure success.
12. True. Everyone needs a chance to show what they can do.
13. False. They are usually capable of much, much more.
14. True. This is the critical connection.
15. True. Too often it is all or nothing.
16. True. Too much interference spoils the results.
17. True. It will make your life much easier.
18. True. And don't you forget it!

TEN TRAPS TO AVOID

Avoid the ten traps listed on the next page.

TEN TRAPS TO AVOID

Check those you intend to avoid.

☐ 1. Thinking you can do everything yourself.

☐ 2. Failing to give employees challenging assignments with enough latitude to handle them.

☐ 3. Careless selection of an authority level when assigning a project.

☐ 4. Overlooking delegation opportunities for untried and untested employees.

☐ 5. Holding on to nonmanagement tasks that someone else could do.

☐ 6. Too little or too much follow-up.

☐ 7. Withholding vital information pertinent to a delegated assignment.

☐ 8. Failure to recognize employee accomplishments.

☐ 9. Overburdening your best, most trusted people because you have not prepared anyone else.

☐ 10. Failing to hold a critique with an employee after the accomplishment of a major task to see what you both have learned.

A DELEGATION CHECKLIST

The following checklist is designed to guide the manager through the delegation process.

1. PERSONAL PREPARATION

I have reviewed my job and analyzed or identified:

_____ my duties and responsibilities
_____ key results areas
_____ objectives
_____ management tasks versus operating work
_____ the assignments I can delegate

2. PLANNING THE DELEGATION

I have planned the delegation and established or considered:

_____ the objectives to be accomplished
_____ completion dates
_____ standards to be met
_____ the decision making required
_____ the amount of authority to be delegated
_____ budget and other resource requirements
_____ how involved I want to be
_____ what feedback I want and when I want it
_____ the person to whom I will delegate

3. SELECTING THE RIGHT PERSON

I have selected an employee after considering:

_____ to whom the work logically belongs
_____ who has the interest or the ability
_____ who will find the work challenging
_____ who the assignment will help develop
_____ who has been overlooked in the past
_____ who is best qualified
_____ who has the time
_____ who will do the best job

4. MAKING THE DELEGATION

When I communicate the delegation I will:

____ describe the task and results expected
____ agree on standards of performance and timetables
____ determine training needs and when training will be provided
____ state the amount and frequency of feedback I expect
____ define parameters and resources, including budgets
____ spell out the level of authority
____ tell others who is in charge

5. FOLLOWING THROUGH

I will follow through by:

____ setting reasonable reporting and review schedules
____ respecting the level of delegation given
____ communicating freely and openly
____ supporting the employee to the extent required
____ offering encouragement and reinforcing employee strengths and abilities
____ recognizing achievement
____ intervening only if *absolutely* necessary

DEVELOP A PERSONAL ACTION PLAN

Think over the material you have read. Review the self-analysis questionnaires and the Missed Opportunities page. Rethink the case studies and the reinforcement exercises. What have you learned about delegation? What have you learned about yourself as a delegator? How can you apply what you have learned? Make a commitment to yourself to become a better delegator and a more effective manager by designing a personal action plan to help you accomplish this goal.

The following guide may help you clarify your goals and outline the actions required to achieve them.

1. My current delegation skills are effective in the following areas:

   ____

   ____

2. I need to improve my delegation skills in the following areas:

   ____

   ____

3. My goals for improving my delegation skills are as follows (be sure they are specific, attainable, and measurable):

   ____

   ____

4. These people are resources who can help me achieve my goals:

   ____

   ____

5. Following are my action steps, along with a timetable to accomplish each goal:

   ____

   ____

RESPONSES TO CASE STUDIES

Case Study 1—The Do-It-Yourself Manager

Joanne's supervisor didn't waste time getting to the point. She simply asked her to talk about her workload and that of her subordinates. The contrast made the problem obvious. When Joanne explained her rationale, the supervisor would not buy it. She suggested Joanne take a good look at her subordinates and their past work record. Most were high achievers when given the chance. She suggested that Joanne was afraid to let go of responsibility and authority and perhaps enjoyed ''doing'' work more than ''managing'' work. Joanne then admitted that perhaps she didn't know how to let go and still maintain control. The discussion concluded with Joanne agreeing to attend a seminar on delegating and to work closely with her supervisor when she was unsure of how to proceed.

Case Study 2—Baffled by the Budget

Jack has to release total control of the budget process in his unit in order to get operating control. He should make key staff members responsible for their part of the budget and hold them accountable for results. This means they should participate in the development of the budget and its day-to-day administration.

Jack's administrative assistant could be assigned responsibility for pulling the tentative budget together with the help and input of the section heads. When they feel it is complete, they can present it to Jack for review and approval and then follow up to see that everyone stays on track.

Case Study 3—Making Choices

It is good that Susan has identified Mary Wong's strengths and is delegating to her. However, she may be delegating so much that Mary is carrying an unfair share of the load and other employees are being prevented from learning new things. Balancing tasks between employees is always difficult, especially when there are one or two you know can do it all and the others would be a risk. You can minimize the risk when assigning work to employees you don't know well by planning the delegation carefully, following up on progress frequently, and training as necessary. Otherwise, you and your "Mary Wongs" will be doing all the important and complex work yourselves and your other employees will be stagnating.

Case Study 4—The Incomplete Data Dilemma

Like many managers, Marla is delegating sufficient authority to capable people to get the work done. Unfortunately, she is not making it clear to everyone involved who is in charge of the investigations, and much of the data input is to her instead of to the employee in charge of the project. In spite of her efforts to translate the information and pass it on quickly, she has become a communications block. Her "translations" may not be accurate, and her intervention prevents the employee who needs the data from asking clarifying questions or requesting additional information. Her employees become defensive when she criticizes them for not handling information well because she is the reason and they are reluctant to say so.

Case Study 5—The Delegation Disaster

Jim is to be commended for realizing the need to delegate, but he moved too quickly and without preparing the people properly.

Jim should have taken the time to get to know each person and to learn something about their needs, abilities, and goals. It would also have been helpful to share his management style and personal goals for the organization. A gradual increase in delegated tasks with employees participating in determining the authority level would have been less threatening to the employees, since they did not seem to understand delegation or have confidence in their ability to undertake new assignments.

NOTES

NOTES

FOR OTHER FIFTY-MINUTE SELF-STUDY BOOKS
SEE THE BACK OF THIS BOOK.

NOTES

FOR OTHER FIFTY-MINUTE SELF-STUDY BOOKS
SEE THE BACK OF THIS BOOK.

NOTES

FOR OTHER FIFTY-MINUTE SELF-STUDY BOOKS
SEE THE BACK OF THIS BOOK.

NOTES

FOR OTHER FIFTY-MINUTE SELF-STUDY BOOKS
SEE THE BACK OF THIS BOOK.

NOTES

FOR OTHER FIFTY-MINUTE SELF-STUDY BOOKS
SEE THE BACK OF THIS BOOK.

NOTES

FOR OTHER FIFTY-MINUTE SELF-STUDY BOOKS
SEE THE BACK OF THIS BOOK.

ABOUT THE FIFTY-MINUTE SERIES

We hope you enjoyed this book and found it valuable. If so, we have good news for you. This title is part of the best selling ***FIFTY-MINUTE Series*** of books. All other books are similar in size and identical in price. Several books are supported with a training video. These are identified by the symbol Ⓥ next to the title.

Since the first ***FIFTY-MINUTE*** book appeared in 1986, more than five million copies have been sold worldwide. Each book was developed with the reader in mind. The result is a concise, high quality module written in a positive, readable self-study format.

FIFTY-MINUTE Books and Videos are available from your distributor or from Crisp Publications, Inc., 95 First Street, Los Altos, CA 94022. A free current catalog is available on request.

The complete list of ***FIFTY-MINUTE Series*** Books and Videos are listed on the following pages and organized by general subject area.

MANAGEMENT TRAINING

	Title	
	Self-Managing Teams	00-0
	Delegating for Results	008-6
	Successful Negotiation — Revised	09-2
Ⓥ	Increasing Employee Productivity	10-8
	Personal Performance Contracts — Revised	12-2
Ⓥ	Team Building — Revised	16-5
Ⓥ	Effective Meeting Skills	33-5
Ⓥ	An Honest Day's Work: Motivating Employees	39-4
Ⓥ	Managing Disagreement Constructively	41-6
	Learning To Lead	43-4
Ⓥ	The Fifty-Minute Supervisor — 2/e	58-0
Ⓥ	Leadership Skills for Women	62-9
Ⓥ	Coaching & Counseling	68-8
	Ethics in Business	69-6
	Understanding Organizational Change	71-8

MANAGEMENT TRAINING (Cont.)

	Title	Code
	Project Management	75-0
	Risk Taking	076-9
	Managing Organizational Change	80-7
V	Working Together in a Multi-Cultural Organization	85-8
	Selecting And Working With Consultants	87-4
	Empowerment	096-5
	Managing for Commitment	099-X
	Rate Your Skills as a Manager	101-5

PERSONNEL/HUMAN RESOURCES

	Title	Code
V	Your First Thirty Days: A Professional Image in a New Job	003-5
	Office Management: A Guide to Productivity	005-1
	Men and Women: Partners at Work	009-4
	Effective Performance Appraisals — Revised	11-4
	Quality Interviewing — Revised	13-0
	Personal Counseling	14-9
	Giving and Receiving Criticism	023-X
	Attacking Absenteeism	042-6
	New Employee Orientation	46-7
	Professional Excellence for Secretaries	52-1
	Guide to Affirmative Action	54-8
	Writing a Human Resources Manual	70-X
	Downsizing Without Disaster	081-7
	Winning at Human Relations	86-6
	High Performance Hiring	088-4

COMMUNICATIONS

	Title	Code
	Technical Writing in the Corporate World	004-3
V	Effective Presentation Skills	24-6
V	Better Business Writing — Revised	25-4
V	The Business of Listening	34-3
	Writing Fitness	35-1
	The Art of Communicating	45-9
	Technical Presentation Skills	55-6
V	Making Humor Work	61-0
	50 One Minute Tips to Better Communication	071-X
	Speed-Reading in Business	78-5
	Influencing Others	84-X

PERSONAL IMPROVEMENT

	Title	Order No.
V	Attitude: Your Most Priceless Possession — Revised	011-6
V	Personal Time Management	22-X
	Successful Self-Management	26-2
	Business Etiquette And Professionalism	32-9
V	Balancing Home & Career — Revised	35-3
V	Developing Positive Assertiveness	38-6
	The Telephone and Time Management	53-X
	Memory Skills in Business	56-4
	Developing Self-Esteem	66-1
	Managing Personal Change	74-2
	Finding Your Purpose	072-8
	Concentration!	073-6
	Plan Your Work/Work Your Plan!	078-7
	Stop Procrastinating: Get To Work!	88-2
	12 Steps to Self-Improvement	102-3

CREATIVITY

	Title	Order No.
	Systematic Problem Solving & Decision Making	63-7
V	Creativity in Business	67-X
	Intuitive Decision Making	098-1

TRAINING

	Title	Order No.
	Training Managers to Train	43-2
	Visual Aids in Business	77-7
	Developing Instructional Design	076-0
	Training Methods That Work	082-5

WELLNESS

	Title	Order No.
V	Mental Fitness: A Guide to Stress Management	15-7
	Wellness in the Workplace	020-5
	Personal Wellness	21-3
	Preventing Job Burnout	23-8
V	Job Performance and Chemical Dependency	27-0
	Overcoming Anxiety	29-9
	Productivity at the Workstation	41-8
	Health Strategies for Working Women	079-5

CUSTOMER SERVICE/SALES TRAINING

	Title	Order No.
	Sales Training Basics — Revised	02-5
	Restaurant Server's Guide — Revised	08-4
	Effective Sales Management	31-0
	Professional Selling	42-4
	Telemarketing Basics	60-2
	Telephone Courtesy & Customer Service — Revised	64-7

CUSTOMER SERVICE/SALES TRAINING (CONT.)

	Title	Code
V	Calming Upset Customers	65-3
V	Quality at Work	72-6
	Managing Quality Customer Service	83-1
	Customer Satisfaction — Revised	84-1
V	Quality Customer Service — Revised	95-5

SMALL BUSINESS/FINANCIAL PLANNING

Title	Code
Consulting for Success	006-X
Understanding Financial Statements	22-1
Marketing Your Consulting or Professional Services	40-8
Starting Your New Business	44-0
Direct Mail Magic	075-2
Credits & Collections	080-9
Publicity Power	82-3
Writing & Implementing Your Marketing Plan	083-3
Personal Financial Fitness — Revised	89-0
Financial Planning With Employee Benefits	90-4

ADULT LITERACY/BASIC LEARNING

Title	Code
Returning to Learning: Getting Your G.E.D.	02-7
Study Skills Strategies — Revised	05-X
The College Experience	07-8
Basic Business Math	24-8
Becoming an Effective Tutor	28-0
Reading Improvement	086-8
Introduction to Microcomputers	087-6
Clear Writing	094-9
Building Blocks of Business Writing	095-7
Language, Customs & Protocol For Foreign Students	097-3

CAREER BUILDING

Title	Code
Career Discovery - Revised	07-6
Effective Networking	30-2
Preparing for Your Interview	33-7
Plan B: Protecting Your Career	48-3
I Got The Job! - Revised	59-9
Job Search That Works	105-8